MW01327671

A Poetic Glimpse of Africa

By

John R. Davison

This book is a work of non-fiction. Names and places have been changed to protect the privacy of all individuals. The events and situations are true.

© 2002 by John R. Davison. All rights reserved.

No part of this book may be reproduced, stored in a retrieval system, or transmitted by any means, electronic, mechanical, photocopying, recording, or otherwise, without written permission from the author.

ISBN: 1-4033-4494-9 (e-book)
ISBN: 1-4033-4495-7 (Paperback)

This book is printed on acid free paper.

1stBooks - rev. 03/28/03

DEDICATION

This book is dedicated to my Aunt, my Aunt Mattie Durant, the lady in my family who has had a tremendous influence in my growth and development and been a positive motivating force in my life.

This book is dedicated to a very strong, sensitive and people serving deeply religious woman, to my Aunt Mattie and to all the Aunt Mattie's everywhere who seem to be present at the right time.

TABLE OF CONTENTS

INTRODUCTION

The poems while having a unique African flavor, reflective of what I actually experienced while living in West Africa, possess a universal message flowing through most of the poems.

I had traveled worldwide, prior to taking up permanent residency in Africa, where I lived for two years. As a professional, accepting the post and assignment to live and work in Africa, I was afforded an opportunity to deal with Nationals or transplanted foreigners, professionals, business people, government officials and Liberians on every level. My organization had sought to prepare us for foreign service and provided a list of do's and don'ts. But, I was unprepared for the vast cultural differences I would experience on the continent of Africa. Liberia has the unique distinction of being the oldest Republic in Africa with strong United States ties. Liberia was established as a Republic by black people; black people, mostly recently emancipated and freed unowned Negro slaves. Slaves who set sail from America and Canada, seeking independence in Liberia, West Africa.

I journeyed to Liberia, West Africa in 1978 and prior to my arrival in Liberia, Liberia had not suffered a major civil war in over one hundred and fifty years. I found it ironic that I should be in this peace enduring country when the bloody coup or over throw of the government took place on April 14, 1980. Liberia is warm, tropical, English speaking and about the size of the state of Ohio with a population just over two million. Living in Liberia was delightful prior to the coup.

While my poems reflect on my observations, it moreover reflect on the lives of my African brothers and sisters, I peacefully lived with for more than two years. The poems depict the daily lives of Liberians and chronicles African history in a factual sense. The poems, historically and factually accurate, reflect on Liberia's struggle for autonomy, her struggle for economic stability, her village life, her tribal life and tribal customs, the friendships I experienced, the kinships I developed, Africa's legitimate frustration, her anger, her fears and indeed her humor. I hope the manner in which I have depicted Africa in the idiom of poetry will be to my readers' liking.

- John R. Davison

FORWARD: BE ENTERTAINED AND BE ENLIGHTENED

This book is unique, in that it has a definite story-like format with a definitive beginning, diversified plot and dramatic ending. Originally, developed as a manuscript for a book, the poems only glean topical matter to be dealt with at length in my subsequent publications.

The African and universal phenomenon dealt with is both intense and serious. While the poems provide snapshots of daily life in Liberia, a little country at the base of the huge western bulge of Africa, the poems keep in perspective Africa's history, while focusing on the diversity of the country's inhabitants. The poems keep in perspective Africa's history, her political phenomenon and her socio-economic phenomenon.

The collective work promises to entertain, intrigue and enlighten you at the same time.

PREFACE

This book was written to inform, educate, entertain and enlighten my readers with respect to African folklore. Hopefully, the reading will increase the readers appreciation for his own heritage.

The idiom of the poem was selected for this initial work because the poetic literary form is enjoyable reading which tends to quickly enlighten and entertain its reading audience.

"A Poetic Glimpse of Africa" is a dramatic snapshot of daily life in Africa. The poetic truths being shared with the readers are based on my first hand experiences and based on my observations while living on the Continent of Africa, taking into account that I traveled to the Ivory Coast and Togo, which are French speaking countries.

The subject matter of the poems deals with some very substantive and serious issues. While the literary quality of the poems gives the poetic work a novel like quality, the African folklore poetized maintains a clear, concise and simplified rhythmic flow from the beginning to the end.

Hopefully, this book will enable the readers to share in the history making events surrounding the country's first major revolution, a revolution I witnessed first hand and indeed survived. Hopefully, the readers will become more enlightened with respect to daily life in Africa as I experienced it.

CHIEFDOMS

In the beginning, an African man
Took one wife and sometimes many
They multiplied, his household grew
And his clan became his family

Several families would form a clan
The clan soon became a village
A strongman would be made Clan Chief
As Clan Chief, he presided over the village

Clans and villages coming together
Established the tribal groups
Tribal groups evolved into a nation
With a Paramount Chief, serving as the supreme ruler

Early man lived outside the dense bush
He lived on cleared land at peace with his neighbors
His only reason for retreating into the bush
Was to escape the grasp of the foreign slave-traders

1

AFRICAN TRIBES

Africans are a diverse people
Africa reportedly has about 2,800 tribes
In Liberia's Western and Central Provinces
Eight or more major tribes, still survive

They are Bandi, Belle, Buzi
They are Mende and Gio
They are Bassa, Krus and Kpelle
And the superbly governed Mandingo

It is said of the Bande
That they are the least aggressive
Bande are gifted in art and dancing
Bande are talented and notably artistic

The Belle are great builders
The Belle are said to be striking and handsome
And the Belle women extraordinary beauty
Is said to flatter the photographer's camera

The Buzi are a border tribe
They occupy the nearby Guinea frontier
The Buzi excel in technology and language
Are known to excel in literature

The Bassa farmers were also great warriors
And played a major role in Liberia's defense
Bassa farmers contributed to Liberia's National growth
Bassa tribesmen were a major force in government

The Mende are a likable people
The Mende live near the border of Sierre Leone
The Mendes excelled in police work and as artisans
The Mende are known to be imaginative and strong

The Mano and Gio are very warm hearted
They possess strong Negroid features and muscular bodies
They believe in tribal doctoring and excel in health care
And value tribal beliefs and the power of prayer

The Krus are great fishermen
And world renowned boatsmen
Krus are a populous coastal people
Known to be warm and very friendly

The Mandingo read and write fluent Arabic
They farm fertile land, breed horses and cattle
Mandingo govern according to Mohammedan law
Are traders, peace loving and not opposed to battle

While Twentieth Century technology ushered in change
Most of tribal Africa remained the same
Tropical rains knocked out power lines, roads became a mudslide
And modern technology, instantly fell to the wayside

Tribal people still communicate, mainly by drum
So modern power devices mean little to them
Power lines, clocks and automobiles
Still have little effect on how village people live

John R. Davison

Constructing a Thatch Hut

John R. Davison

BIRTH OF A VILLAGE

Center Pole is erected

Frame around the pole

Framing around the center pole

7

John R. Davison

A NEW TRIBAL VILLAGE IS BORN

VILLAGE PEOPLE

You're walking, you pass a black woman
Walking down an unpaved country road
As she strolls by, you catch her smile
She is regally clad in a multi colored robe

She transports a filled kerosene lantern
That she balances on her head with ease
The lamp will provide an entire village light
Ordinarily darkened by the night's soaring trees

You also pass a tribal postman
His mail pouch rest atop his head
Centered on the pouch is a water jug
In his bare feet, he crosses a narrow bridge

You pass a tribal hunter
Clad in brief-like underwear
He peddles freshly killed antelope and buffalo
The animals' blood color the metal of his spear

Passing through the village, you rest a moment
You see village women busy at work
While they work, children play together
In front of their home, a clay thatch roofed hut

The hour is late, approaching palaver time
It's getting dark, villagers gather near the main hut
The major meal is ready to be served
The total serving is called "**country chop**"

Peanuts, pineapple, fruits and berries
Are richly flavored with palm oil
Dryland rice and sometimes pod peppers
Are combined in the kettle pot to boil

9

John R. Davison

Soaring silhouette palms sway with the breeze
You listen to the sound of tribal drums
In time, the loud chatter, singing and laughter
Subsides with the darkness and all blend into one

THE GAMES VILLAGERS PLAY

John R. Davison

VILLAGE PEOPLE

DRUMS

Drum songs tell of life
Drum songs tell when someone dies
Drum songs say, a little baby comes
Drum songs say to all, come and eat rice

Drums say, do a war dance
Drum songs causes you to shiver
Drum songs say you must keep quiet
Drums say friends palaver(meet & talk)upriver

Drums say an old one is sick
Drums call the little ones home
Drums can summon one and all to meet
Drums speak in many dialects and tongues

War size drums are very large
War drums alert villagers of a fire
Double headed drums are held under the arm
Are beaten by hand and move you to dance

Talking drums are often small
And shaped like hour glasses
They are always beaten with a stick
They are always beaten, while being carried

Drums have tribal names
Drum language is always well coded
Drums speak many dialects
Drums enchant you and tell many stories

John R. Davison

TRIBAL MEDICINE

Tribal drum songs compel attention
When summoning the Medicine man
The Zo, the village native physician
Always comes to doctor those in pain

Two tribal youths playfully wrestled
The Bassa youth was violently thrown
The youth slightly regarded his injury
Diagnosed by the Zo, as a broken foot bone

A white doctor from a nearby mission
Prescribed a plaster-of-paris splint
But, because the native specialist was highly regarded
The mission doctor conceded treatment to him

The tribal doctor massaged the foot daily
A hardening astringent was daily applied
The youth walked lightly, and about a week later
He had no limp or deformity, his foot healed fine

The tribal doctor routinely concocts
Medicinal herbs and effective disinfectants
And prepares a variety of native leaf potions
That effectively drains and cures most abscesses

Fevers, the Zo effectively treats
Having his patients drink hot and bitter lemon teas
And the sick hut, serves to isolate measles victims
As well as those with other communicable diseases

Liniments and ointments, the Zo concocts
Believed to cure most common skin rashes
Watered soft clay from ant hills he
skillfully mixes with insects formic acid

The treatment prescribed a rheumatoid patient
Is to massage them and give them a liniment rub
They are prostrated on a bed of heated leaves
And for several days, kept warmly covered

This passed down age old proven remedy
The patient always warmly receives
And is believed to provide the rheumatoid patient
Long periods of relaxing and therapeutic relief

Early tribal doctors practiced
Now outlawed Jungle-edge psychotherapy
Later condemned as a punishable form of medicine
This practice was outlawed as illegal and unhealthy

The medicine prescribed an insolent woman
Often avoided, because of her loud mouth
Was a bitter leaf drinking potion the Zo prepared
With an odor that was extremely foul

The awful stench of the imbibed potion
Left the woman with such a lasting foul breath
That her breath whenever she exhaled it
Offended everyone and the woman herself

While deemed illegal and unorthodox medicine
A prescription offensive to enlightened men
The treatment more often proved curative
Consistently curing the diarrhetic mouth problem

John R. Davison

"The Struggle"

As a Nation, we continue to struggle
Struggle, to deal with adversity and strife
We struggle for peace and harmony
We struggle for a better life

But, it is difficult in Africa
Where growth and progress are slow
Where daily survival is a never ending struggle
Where ninety percent of the people are illiterate and poor

The years I lived on the African Continent
I learned much about African folklore
Her main exports were U. S. produced rubber
And German mined iron ore

These exports, about sixty percent of her trade
Didn't balance her budget or offset her debts
So Africa remained a captive state
Beholding to foreign powers, she could not pay

There is milled lumber and oil refining
Coffee, cocoa and semi precious stones mining
There is palm oil, sugar cane and home grown rice
Mostly government processed and indeed overpriced

The government runs key factories
And control the production of flour, sugar and dry fish
These staples make up the diet of her people
And are hard to cook and often hard to get

The Country began to prosper in about 1830
People idolized their then President
Monrovia, the city then a village of ninety dwellings
Had less than seven hundred residents

16

Monrovia, the city in1980, had over 250,000 residents
The city flourished and started rural projects
Over 300,000 Liberians worked for the government

Free Zoning began to attract foreign merchants
The merchants were enticed like rats to cheese
The government offered short range tax incentives
Aware it was dealing with long range thieves

Free Zone foreign skilled merchants
Knew how to manipulate and contrive
And to how to wheel and deal to turn a profit
And buy officials, receptive to their bribes

The President's hand was in almost everything
His stock ownership often was fifty percent
The President amassed very huge fortunes
Storing his illegally received loot in foreign banks

If the President's interest faltered
He always denied his share of the cost
He'd publicly reprimand his foreign partner
And refuse to share in the loss

World Bank loans and foreign gifts
Gave this emerging economy a needed lift
It was sound diplomacy and not African politics
That brought on the prosperity of 1976

In Monrovia, a University was built
As was an arena for soccer and competitive sports
A city court system, new school and hotels went up
As did miles of new highways and an International Airport

The government spent eighty eight million dollars
To establish six thousand miles of new roads
Village people crowded into the city
There was a forty two percent unemployment role

Rice prices soared, by Presidential decree
The impoverished masses rebelled
They protested in public and armed soldiers reacted
Many were injured and forty protestors were killed

Five hundred or so were seriously injured
Thirty five million in property was destroyed
Some 137,000 rural rice growers voiced their anger
And they swore to die, rather than be ignored

Troops from neighboring Guinea were called in
By a desperate and frightened Liberian President
The rice price increase was serious business
The situation was indeed intense

The President publicly blamed foreign merchants
For the riot and severe property loss
And he publicly denied that he had profited
From farming rice and increasing rice costs

April the fourteenth, one year later
A well executed coup was ordered
The President and his entire Cabinet
By the military regime, were brutally slaughtered

"Tale of Two Liberian Presidents"

Two intelligent Liberian Statesmen
Brought to the Office of President
Progressive and enlightened leadership
And a mature and noble-like presence

They promoted manufacturing the main staples
They expanded commerce and foreign banking relations
The promoted economic growth and expanded trade
and government subsidized education

The government was burdened with enormous loans
Their foreign debt became to much to manage
So the price of staples like rice and taxes were raised
Creating a situation the leadership couldn't handle

The masses protested and voiced their opposition
The Presidents exercised dictatorial discretion
Those opposed were charged with illegal collusion
Some were threatened and many imprisoned and arrested

The oppressive action brought on civil violence
Riotous mobs swept over Monrovia and the Mansion
The fleeting Presidents were quickly apprehended
They were brutally assaulted, as their lives were ended

The violence taking place and the ensuing mayhem
Placed Africa's first Republic in International disfavor
It ended two Liberian Presidents' infamous rule
Edward James Royce in 1871 and William Tolbert rule in 1980

"Sandcrabs"

Sandcrabs seem by nature endowed
With strong survival traits
Thy never ride waves out to sea
They instinctively know, in this, there is no escape

Sandcrabs race toward outgoing ragging tides
And seem to invite the ragging tide's return
But, in the blink of an eye, they burrow in the sand
And avoid the tides grasp, in the nick of time

In life, We often imitate sandcrabs
And invite life's consuming and ragging tides
And if we fail to timely anchor ourselves
Like the sandcrab, We will not survive

"African American Connection"

The Stand together leadership in 1920
Thrived under President Charles B. King
His Leadership won Tribal Liberians full support
And brought tribesmen into the mainstream

With a worldwide depression approaching
And African foreign trade at its lowest ebb
President King started self-help programs
Much like those of President Franklin Roosevelt

By 1930, the African economy
Was on the brink of collapse
Foreign aide was not available
Government debts could not be met

Edwin Barclay, Liberia's 18th President
Was indeed a colorful Head of State
He waged a war on the dreaded diseases
Diseases his people regularly faced

Barclay had watched expecting mothers
Labor with their baby on the way
He watched them in pain for want of medicine
He watched them die, where they lay

Tuberculosis, then a major killer
In Africa ranked with malaria and leprosy
So Barclay rallied the support of his people
To stamp out these dreaded diseases

President Barclay appealed to Liberians
To abandon tribal medicine as a cure
In 1928, by Presidential decree
He established the Public Health Bureau

Barclay denounced Germany Hitler's scrapping
Of the Treaty at Versailles, France in 1933
He denounced Germany's colonial abandonment of Africa
And defended Liberia's stand on neutrality

Throughout World War II
Barclay appealed for America's assistance
But, with no Embassy in Washington, D.C.
His efforts only met with resistance

In 1940, World War II escalated
Germany was winning and clearly ahead
Germany needed landing airstrips in Africa
Germany badly needed this critical edge

America struck a bargain with Liberia
America agreed to construct Airstrips on Firestone's land
In 1942, the air base construction was underway
Engineers and U. S. Negro troops were brought in

Experts predicted a Nazi Germany sweeping annihilation
Many predicted that all of Africa would die
But, the U. S. built Airstrips insured a U. S. victory
And served well, the U. S. and U. S. allies

The U. S. offered to protect its air bases
And to protect U. S. facilities and traveled inroads
The U. S. built Liberian airstrips in a dozen places
And established for Liberia an International Airport

Major peacetime construction took place
Both in the U. S. and abroad
And a grateful America did not forget
The role Liberia and Africa played in the War

America aided Africa
And funded Africa's peacetime development
Agreeing to employ local African labor

In spite of voiced worldwide resentment

At the hands of skilled Liberian Tribesmen
Liberia was nationally transformed
Tribesmen built factories, plants and paved roads
An historical fact, not widely known

This small Liberian Nation
Was thrust into the air age
Even before, Liberia had vehicles
For the roads newly paved

About two thousand tribesmen
Trained and equipped with many skills
Operated tractors, bulldozers and cranes
As the docks and railroad were built

Through dense forest and through swamp hinterlands
Trains in Liberia transported rubber and rich ore
But, financial backing, still a major problem
Remained to be explored

The road to Mecca
Is not paved with silver and gold
And it seemed, the railroad would not be finished
Or successfully move the rich ore

But, somehow the Christie project succeeded
And on April 16th in 1951
Iron ore, by train reached deep water harbor
The railroad witnessed a successful run

President Tubman served six consecutive terms
And for twenty six years, Tubman ruled supreme
His blunder with Firestone's strikers, notwithstanding
As Liberia's President, he was held in great esteem

John R. Davison

SOCCER GAMES

Tribal School
for young boys

MY VILLAGE, MY TRIBE

John R. Davison

"My Village, My Tribe"

We are village people, in a one room house
A shelter of cinder blocks and roof covered with zinc
As neighbors, we walk freely about
And share with each other, the important things

We don't care about a radio or TV
Or desire a phone or stereo
We can't afford the electricity anyway
We can't afford to have rugs on our floors

We cook on an outside coal pot
Draw water from a nearby well
And when the nights are very hot
Our sweating bodies, we freely bare

Crude furniture, we construct by hand
Our walls and floors are bare
Fufu, our main dish is soaked overnight
No cushions line our homemade chairs

We embrace our culture
The traditional way
Our Parents and our Elders
We respect and obey

We rise at daybreak
And wash in nearby streams
And practice religion and medicine
As tribal custom deems

Our young men, we prepare for manhood
For womanhood, our young women are prepared
By tribal laws, all our people are bound
By laws denied outsiders to hear

Ritualistic sacrifice, may bring you fame
And it may also bring you status and wealth
Ritualistic sacrifice brings always pain
And for some, a quick and certain death

John R. Davison

"For One Woman, One Man"

In this land of many wives for each man
Are strong women with their own point of view
Some call them bossy, frisky and mean
And regard them as the well to do

These African women often own much land
And run the family business
Are often educated abroad
And demand peer recognition

This woman will deal confidently with her mate
And will handle as confidently affairs of State

Home chores, she will seldom delegate
She alone will cook and wash and bake

She teaches her girl child at an early age
The many roles in life she must learn to play

Her man often works outside their home
His work may involve about anything
But, at home he never lifts a hand
At home, he is treated as a king

I came to know such women
In this distant tropical land
And to appreciate their tenacity
For they too, are African

"Women's Society"

Virginity is precious and highly valued
In this far away and distant land
Where livestock and grain are still exchanged
For a neighbor's daughter hand

Some seek a wife, who wants it regularly
Some a wife wanting it once in a while
Some seek a wife wanting it, when he wants it
But, all seek a wife to bear many a child

A girl is taught by tribal custom
That she exist to satisfy her husband
At an appointed time, a girl is taken away
And she may be gone for several days

The girls initiation is a ceremonial event
Held in the Society's secret place
During initiation, virgin girls become spell bound
So, the old people say

The young initiate is taught the ways of men
And the ways of women, she must now understand
She is taught about the powers of roots and herbs
And about life saving minerals beneath the earth

She is taught how to delay a pregnancy
And how to bring a pregnancy on
And if there is no help around
She is taught how to deliver alone, her newborn

She learns how to treat a minor illness
And how to treat a sore or bruise
And how to clean and dress her body
And with straw, weave the family's shoes

29

"Women's Society (continued)"

The final rite to be performed
It the highpoint of the initiating ceremony
For this girl, who was only a naive child
Will soon become a woman

Preparing the body, is carefully done
For her virginity is a cherished gift
A herbal solution is ritualistically applied
To the area, where the clitoris will be clipped

For several days, the girl remains crazed and out of sorts
And thrashes feverishly about
And older girlfriend is constantly at her side
To help her sort things out

The initiated girl in time fully comes around
And the Society of Women understand
She is now ready to be wedded
And be easily aroused by her man

A second girl is next prepared
Her clitoris is totally removed
She screams with pain and bleeds profusely
The healing solution is applied to her wound
Her future will be with an older man
Who wants it just once in a while
The joy of arousal, for her won't exist
And she will often be with child

The third girl, escapes before being initiated
Her mind and body are left alone
No man will have a claim on her
Her sexuality will be all her own
She will have no part in a dowry marriage
And have nothing to do with the Women's Society
She will select her men and decide her lifestyle
And might choose to never be with child

DANCE

DANCE

John R. Davison

"For One Man, Many Wives"

Africa is a land, where often a man
Is allowed to take several wives
He takes on more, than just bodily pleasures
He becomes responsible for their well being and lives

He will be their lifetime provider
And he must provide in every way
He must provide food, clothing shelter
And conjugal night-time play

Each wife will use her special talent
To meet the family needs

One wife will work in the marketplace
Behind a well stocked stand
Selling clothes and novel things
Thing, often made by hand

One wife will cook meals
For the entire family to share
And wash all the clothes
That the entire family wear

One wife might be well endowed
With a sensual bosom and sensual behind
Always eager to please her man
When it's love making time

One wife might delight in greeting
Her husband with a gracious smile
And take pleasure and great joy
In bearing many a child

SWEET TING

John R. Davison

"SWEET TING"

Who is this sensual being
Whose clothes so tightly cling
She has no restricted body movements
Perhaps, she wears no under-things

With a piece of colored fabric
She creates a headdress befitting a Queen
And with another piece of fabric
She regally gowns her total being

Her dress while tight, is long and hitting
With splits strategically placed
Her healthy hair is braided evenly
It silhouette's her sculptured face

She wears well, gold in abundance
Chains, bracelets and assorted rings
Her rhythmic walk enchants you
African men call her 'Sweet Ting'

Her feminine ways intrigue you
Whether she is heavy, plump or thin
This sensual being of whom I speak
Embodies all that is African

"Outside Child"

It is the custom for an African father
To have the sons he father carry his name
His many offsprings, outside his marriage
Are by law his namesake, for life to claim

Fathers are an honored and dominant force
Especially during early boyhood years
Fathers take custody as a legal right
A right, they may not with the mother share

A boy born outside of marriage
In time, will learn of his mother's tribe
He will travel by choice to his mother's village
And learn how his mother's people survive

A former Ambassador and government official
Lived less than a hundred yards from me
His outside child, often worked in the yard
Working in my yard, the lad I'd often see

The youth, also worked as his Dad's houseboy
And sometimes, at his Dad's distant farm
The youth's playtime was very limited
He attended school off and on

At age fifteen, he was gone several months
Curious, I inquired why
I was told he'd been summoned upcountry
By the Elders of his mother's tribe

The youth returned from upcountry months later
The boy seemed of a different mind
He bore tribal marking on his cheeks
And markings on his chest and arms

35

The youth had been initiated by his mother's tribe
He was now a man, according to tribal law
This once innocent youth, that I once knew
Was clearly, no longer a boy

He had survived the test of fire
And the test of pain and near death
He was to become a Tribal Chief, I was told
And join the ranks of the Tribal Elders

The Youth's relationship with his father
Would never be the same
And the sum of his father's inheritance
Would only be his father's last name

"CHARITY"

Life is indeed, more precious than gold
It is a gift from God, we must cherish
We must learn to be charitable and freely give
And strive to operate within His Will

The world's well wishers cheer
When good women and men try
And the whole world loses
When good women and men die

We live in a world
To be shared with all others
And we honor God when we share
With our needy sisters and brothers

John R. Davison

"Early Comers - Late Comers"

'Early Comers'

The first African Americans to journey to Africa
Journeyed to Liberia in about 1842
Freed slaves, they met with disease and rejection
But, they managed to make it through

'Late Comers'

The late comers journeying to Liberia
Included me in early 1978
I also faced malaria and problems
But, I also decided to stay

'Early Comers'

The early comers, came in search of liberty
They were learned, skilled and they cared
They were free Americans of Negroid descent
The early comers skin was very fair

'Late Comers'

Late comers came as able administrators
And were skilled technicians too
And while Americans of Negro descent
They looked like Liberians too

'Early Comers'

The early comers met with tropical disease
They caught malaria, were weakened and many died
But, the survivors declared Liberia their home
And they absorbed themselves into twenty three tribes

'Late Comers'

The late comers also caught malaria
But, they were healthy and prepared
They were visionaries with a mission
They functioned free of doubt and fear

'Early Comers"

The early comers battled the odds
And molded a mighty Nation
They governed as compassionate patriarchs
Their lineage now spans more than eight generations

'Late Comers'

Late comers also faced hardship
In spite of their power and wealth
And while committed, sociable and friendly
They stayed mostly to themselves

We are a people bent on freedom
Whether African in Africa or American blacks
And while our culture and beliefs may vary
As victims of racism, we share a common past

A handful of American born Negro settlers
Today govern Liberia's citizens lives
Now in the midst of devastation, poverty and inflation
They struggle as a Nation and barely survive

Two World Wars brought us together
And strengthened our Continental ties
We've maintained the bond through difficult times
Keeping the dream of democracy yet alive

People of color, continue to struggle
Blacks want full citizenship and want it now
Blacks want humane treatment, not based on color
Blacks want worldwide racist regimes struck down

John R. Davison

"Newcomers"

At first, It felt strange, me being there
On that distant coastal shore
Embracing a culture, so totally different
From everything, I had ever known

Liberians greeted me warmly
Their smiles of welcome were many
To them, my dollar meant a lot
And they thought that I had plenty

Was it my manner of speech
Or perhaps my style of clothes
That signaled loud and clear to them
That I was from a distant shore

I checked into my home, the town hotel
It was cheap, but not too sleazy
I climbed three flights to reach the room
A room large and drab and breezy

My room began to feel like a cell
From it, I functioned in every way
I was overjoyed when I found a house
Six months of myself, I relocated in a day

"Just Like Home"

The years I lived in Africa
I lived as one among friends
They resembled me and I resembled them
I was regarded as family, as one among my kin

Africans are unpredictable people
I found it difficult to figure them out
Being among them, I felt a sameness
The sameness, I felt in America's melting pot

I admit, I have seldom witnessed
People, so determined to emulate and be
So much like me, their recent arrival
Who's ancestors crossed earlier this very same Sea

We may be from different cultures now
But, we dream the selfsame dream
We dream of equality and of being free
Having a fulfilled life, it seems

The sunrises slowly, a rooster crows
Outside water is heated on a coal pot stove
Assembled naked, together the family bathes
The wife holds a small mirror, as her husband shaves

Hot tea has can milk added
Sugar is added, to sweeten its taste
Fresh baked shortbread is passed around
And everyone eats in haste

Men leave for work
Or to find a job, for jobs are few
All the children wear school uniforms
And all children walk to school

"Just Like Home (continued)"

Marketplace women sell dry goods and fresh produce
From ground level stands in the open marketplace
If you drive your car to shop, you waste a lot of gas
If you walk, there is hardly walking space

Newborns and infants sleep peacefully
Bundled to their mother's back
While older siblings play on the ground
Confined to the space on a small piece of fabric

Whether inside the store building
Or at her stand, stationed curbside
A mother will bare her naked breast
To feed her hungry child

The marketplace stays crowded
Marketplace women earnings are very small
Store Merchants must honor price controls
And honor government imposed price laws

Tuition while small, all parents must pay
For all their children who attend school
There are no free books or free education
Parents must buy uniforms and buy books too

Family gardens seldom produce growth
It's either too dry or there is too much rain
The struggle to survive seems to never end
But, the struggle is never considered in vain

"AFRICAN SUNSET"

The evening sun's stark brightness
Breaks through a cluster of clouds
And holds you with such intensity
It strains your naked eyes

Towards evening, drifting clouds gather
In clustering shades of white and gray
They shield out the sun and join together
To bring to a close, the light of day

The winding coastline fades away
You can't tell where the coastline starts and ends
The only thing that is visible or heard
Is the rushing tides and the gusting winds

Drifting clouds part briefly and reveal the setting sun
Whitish blue skies become a darkened blue
A dim circular glow, now surrounded by stars
Ushers in a full moon, that mesmerizes you

The ocean and tides loose their furor
And become quiet and very calm
The sun descends below the horizon
The moon in its splendor, signals that the day is gone

John R. Davison

"SLAVERS"

Slavers not only uprooted and stole God's people
But, trespassed on the enslaved God's given space
They disrupted the enslaved genetic continuity
And destroyed the enslaved 's Nation State

Slavers were Portuguese and European
British, German and French
Slavers comprised a score of other
Internationally trespassing and thieving men

Slavers greed made them vicious criminals
And created international distrust
And allowed them to pass on a cruel legacy
Causing present day generations to suffer

Men and women, who see fit to enslave others
Will themselves, never be free women or men
And they are destined to live with the constant fear
That the descendents of the enslaved will get the upper hand

Slavers' octopus-like hold on their captives
And on countries in the Pacific
Failed horribly and miserably
And proved to be costly and risky

Tropical diseases and drinking water problems
Was made worse by the cultural differences
The water, food and language barriers
Made occupation even more hazardous

The Lesson to be learned, is that genetic differences
Agrees with men being in a designated time and space
And any attempts to enslave other free human beings
Offends the laws of God and God's laws of nature

"OH MOTHERLAND"

Motherland, Oh Motherland
Of sand and rust colored clay
Of soaring palms and broad coastlines
Near shores once garrisoning slaves

Oh Motherland, Oh Motherland
Please ease our troubled minds
And bring us peace and serenity
And a love for all mankind

Help us rid our coastal shores
Of exploiters and foreign thieves
Of poverty and illiteracy
And curable common diseases

How valid is National development
When so little we grow and export
Compelled to solicit outside help
To promote our National growth

Too often, we loose
In this game of chance
For the partner we choose
Has the upper hand

He has skilled workers and technicians
And an abundance of capital to invest
And worldwide marketplace influence
Things essential to success

Accepting foreign assistance
Is about as rewarding
As taking an antidote
Before being poisoned

Jobs are scarce
And the pay is small
Pay of $5.00 a day or less
Is not unusual at all

Motherland, Oh Mother Land
We pray for Africa to someday become
Truly independent and a self-sustaining entity
Truly independent, resilient and strong

A County united in her purpose
In control of her own destiny
Efficient and effective in Nation building
And a people who are truly free

"BUSH, IN THE BUSH"

One never speaks of the interior
In West Africa as the Jungle
You say you're going into the bush to visit
Or going to visit your kinfolks upcountry

Upcountry people work the land
And they do few things in haste
They garden and hunt for their food
Things are hand made and there is little waste

Village people follow simple laws
And regard highly their Village Chief
Village Chiefs use their governmental connections
And help their villagers in times of dire need

The journey from the bush to the Capitol city
Involves a very rough and bumpy taxi ride
You share a taxi, you charter with four others
You pray the roads you travel, will be paved and dry

Rainy season brings torrential rains
Washes out dirt roads and floods many villages
You see roadside vehicles, abandoned and ditched
Leaving the Bush, involves many risks

"UNCLE DILLON"

I had been less than nine months in Africa
When Uncle Dillon adopted me
Uncle Dillon often came to my workplace
He was always cheerful and a delight to see

Uncle Dillon wanted me to become his business partner
He shared his dreams with me
He was certain he would find precious diamonds
If I covered the taxi transport and other fees

I learned I was to supply the transport fee
And supply other things as well
Money for needed provisions
To include food, drink and shotgun shells

Our promising partnership beginning
Came to a very sad and abrupt end
Uncle Dillon died a month after returning from upcountry
I lost Uncle Dillon and a very dear friend

Gathering diamonds from downhill streams
Involved game hunting, so it seemed

Uncle Dillon was persistent, so I funded the venture
But, I funded the venture just for fun
A week went by, then two and then three weeks
Before Uncle Dillon and his friend returned

They returned with several precious stones
He and his partner had found
They turned over all the stones to me
Saying, the diamonds, the three of us owned

"NIGHT SOUNDS IN AFRICA"

Night sounds inside Africa's interior
Sound uncomfortably close and different
The sounds penetrate your total being
And compel your total attention

Tribal medicine men roam at nighttime
In search of human parts for juju
You dare not to roam, where the juju man goes
For fear, he might capture you

John R. Davison

"WHEN THE LIGHT GO OUT"

I assembled in the backyard one night
With a group of visiting stateside friends
Suddenly, there was an area-wide electrical blackout
We could not even see our outstretched hands

Neither my security guard on duty
Nor my iron rails or bolted doors
Made us feel, in any measure
That we were safe, protected or secure

These power failures would occur often
When they occurred, you wanted to be home
To unplug all your electrical things
Sure to burn out, when the power surged back on

"Car Boys"

The Nightlife scene in Africa
Brings hundreds into the downtown disco bars
And outside, crowd young carboys
Who charge a quarter to watch out for your car

It is a carboy's fantasy to someday chauffeur
He will clean your windows and hold open your door
He will stay with the car throughout the night
He is often homeless with no place to go

Carboys are youths who have left their small villages
Who have journeyed hundred of miles for a better life
But, the quarters they hustle, barely buy food
Yet, in spite of it all, they seem to survive

John R. Davison

"THE DANCE"

Nightlife for me, when I lived in Africa
Was for me, an awful lot of fun
The Disco rated with New York's finest
You partied from dusk to dawn

The People you'd meet at the disco
Are always friendly and polite
Women greatly outnumbered men
A man rarely brings his wife

The dance floor is always crowded
But, nobody seemed to care
You perspire a lot, your bodies touch
There is excitement in the air

The disc jockey might change the music
From American rock to a tribal dance
A group of African lovely women assemble
And begin a tribal dance and chant

You notice a similarity in body moves
You recognize the unique dance style
Black folks in the U. S. dance this way
You feel like you are suddenly states-side

With Africans, you sense a definite kinship
A familiarity you simply cannot ignore
You see mirrored moods and familiar attitudes
Among Africans, identical to yours

"WHO IS BETTER OFF"

Am I secure in my stately house
With rogue bars, locks
With gated fences
And a live guard about

Sometimes, I think I'd be better off
With neighbors friendly and close
Where nobody has rogue bars and gates
And double locks on all their doors

What of my electric stove
My electric washer and refrigerator
Am I better off having electric appliances
Than my coal pot using neighbor

When the electric power fails
And I loose all sense of order
I quickly revert to coal pot cooking
And washing in rain barrel water

Is it really better to purchase foodstuff
That to preserve, you must refrigerate
Or is it better to daily prepare what you eat
Resigned to prepare your meal on a daily basis

Why pay for a home telephone
Few people have phones, so who will you call
Telephone fees are costly, phones seldom work
So by having a phone, are you really better off

John R. Davison

"TAXI DRIVER"

I like driving my taxi
When driving, I feel free
I drive and listen to nighttime radio
My girl is often sitting next to me

I have no air conditioning
I have no dispatch radio
Windows jam, door handles break
Passengers often slam my doors

Riders squeeze in like sardines in a can
Raising their knees close to their chests
Riders take turns leaning forward
Allowing one another to take a quick deep breath

For his monthly pay of eight dollars
Eight hundred and thirty, the driver must make
He must pay twenty-five daily to the taxi owner
And dash or pay dollars often, to cops on the take

Riders seldom talk to each other
Except in bossy tones
Policemen as passengers never pay a fare
And they claim the front seat as their very own

Your cab accommodates four riders
But, five passengers often crowd in
Your complaints, they simply ignore
And so the journey begins

Passengers are rude to the drivers who are mostly foreigners
Drivers are denied a political point of view
Drivers are verbally abused and criticized
No matter what they say or do

If your taxi breaks down or it fails you
Fares owed you, the passengers will not pay
The passengers will not even help you
Get the taxi off the street or highway

Mechanical failures embarrass you
Good mechanics are far and few
Road Service does not even exist
And would be mechanics have few tools

The taxi owner rarely has insurance
Police stop your taxi all the time
Some riders will not pay their fare
And to argue with them is a waste of time

All you need is one small accident
The accident may not be your fault
But, it will cost you your license and pocket cash
And put you at the mercy of the law

Your taxi will be confiscated
You'll spend time in jail, awaiting bail
You hope number #1, the taxi owner shows up
You hope he stands your bail

He will show to claim his taxi
And sometimes stand your bail
And if he restores your driver's license
Forget about being paid the rest of the year

John R. Davison

"FIGHTING"

Africans never fistfight in public
Street fighting and swearing in public is forbidden
The African way of getting even
Is to savor the flavor of sweet revenge

In the workplace, a situation developed
Where boyhood friends worked together
The college educated friend quickly excelled
While his uneducated brother, did not do well

The work relationship worsened
And the Director decided to cut costs
The educated friend, now the boss
Was directed to issue letter of lay-off

The uneducated friend begged and pleaded
That he be kept on and given one more chance
But, his boyhood friend, his boss said coldly
I've gotta let you go, my man

His friend swore he would get even
His friend replied, yeah and you will rot in jail
His angry friend, hoisted him up in the air
And held him over the balcony rail

We all watched in stark amazement
We being five strong and able bodied men
And it took the sum of our combined strength
To finally separate these two boyhood friends

Had we not acted quickly
And separate this friend and foe
One or both would have fatally descended
To the ground, several stories below

"FIGHTING BACK"

In the year of 1821, Denmark Vessey
A former American born Virginian slave
Gallantly organized a fighting force
A force of more than 9,000 armed Negroes

Vessey's militia armed themselves
With daggers, knives and bayonets
And set out to overthrow their slave masters
By launching a successful slave revolt

Denmark Vessey planned revolt was sabotaged
And fearful whites armed themselves, throughout the South
Whites enacted Jim Crow laws and suppressed Negroes
Whites commissioned ships to ship Negroes out

[many stayed, but a few Negroes left America]

Crossing the Atlantic Ocean, the settlers struggled
They faced tropical disease and hostile African tribes
Farmland could not be tilled, water made them sick
Many were disease stricken and many died

The survivors became friendly with coastal tribes
And received sporadic support from U. S. Naval patrols
They fought off slave traders and slave traders' supporters
Eventually the Negro settlers' colony began to grow

The colony grew to about four hundred strong
A settlers' colony government was eventually formed
A Negro Advisory Council established black control
And the land issue in Lott Carey was cooperatively cleared to farm

The newly formed colony was name **Liberia**
Expanding in 1822 from two miles to 150 square miles
Working the land became a friendly joint venture

Peace existed between the Negro settlers and the tribes

A God fearing Lott Carey kept the settlement going
The settlement accommodated the recaptured slaves
Without a police force, they lived in peace
Many contended, because they fervently prayed

Lott Carey set out, to combat slave trading
He received aid from the U.S. Navy and Marines
Slavers' villages were attacked and burned down
Slavers fled for their lives, never again to be seen

The Liberian bloody War of Liberation
Brought slave trading to an abrupt end
Negro Leadership took hold, the colony expanded
Joseph Jenkins at age 36, became Liberia's first President

"Commonwealth vs. Colony"

For a governed body to become a commonwealth
It must be politically organized as a community
It must have elected officials and be independent
With National goals and a sense of National Unity

For a government to rule as a Republic
The Republic has to be seen by others as a peer
The Republic must govern itself and supply its needs
And have friendly allies, allies it need not fear

Being a colony of uprooted American settlers
Was like being an out-of-wedlock child
You knew you had rights, blood ties and a voice
But, you had no claim to legally enforce

Nineteenth century Africa and especially Liberia
Believed liberation was within her grasp
But, her total dependence on foreign assistance
Prevented Liberation from coming to pass

Forty- nine of Africa's fifty-one countries
Would declare their independence at a future date
And many would be like immature children
Unprepared to deal effectively with the Affairs of State

John R. Davison

"What To Do America"

What to do about ten million in America
People frightened and confused in the year 1810
One third of your people are emancipated slaves
You argue to ship them out, they argue to remain

'What to Do America?'

What to do America
About your newly emancipated slaves
Negroes with skin so fair and straight black hair
Who don't seem to know their place

'What to Do America?'

What will you do America with 800,000 Negroes
Being shipped back to Africa, they totally reject
Trying to colonize them, like England did in Sierre Leone
Would only create an enormous government debt

'What to Do America?'

What to do America
An industrial revolution is at hand
Your Yankee government and European immigrants
Have declared slave labor and slave profiteering
As totally unacceptable and totally un-American

'What to Do America?'

What to do America
Northerners and Southerners don't agree
On anti-slavery and abolitionist ploys
To rid America of slavery
'What to Do America?"

What to do **Christian** America
Your rich humanitarians are ready to spend
And ship emancipated Negroes to distant African shores
Christian America wants its conscious cleansed

'What to Do America?'

What to do America
Blacks **won't exodus** as you planned
Their slave labor, shaped the American landscape
And these former slaves fair share, they demand

"Division and Downfall"

Slave owning states practiced state sovereignty
Completely ignoring Federal anti-slavery laws
They showed no regard for freed Negroes rights
Rights recognized mostly, in the believed free North

Un-owned Negroes living in **slave free** states
Kept their feet off **slave states'** soil
The Dred Scott decision, established as law for Negroes
That they would not receive justice in any American Court

The Missouri Compromise, and Missouri's entry as a territory
Sanctioned both slavery and anti-slavery laws
A freed man could be a **slave** in **St. Louis, Missouri**
And a **slave** could be a **freeman** in **St. Louis, Illinois**

While slavery was clearly unconstitutional
And in violation of the United States laws
Slavers profiteering remained in its hay day
And un-owned Negroes were justifiably outraged

Allowing States to violate anti-slavery laws
Questioned the integrity of our Highest Court
And established a destructive Supreme Court precedent
Unpopular in both the South and the North

Industrial growth started to take hold up North
As European immigrants fled to America's shores
Immigrants came in search of jobs and freedom
America's slavery made these immigrants feel insecure

The United States needed a National militia
To prepare for an impending Mexican War
Anti-slavery proponents wanted new territories **slave free**
This became an issue, dividing the South and the North

The mounting tensions between the South and the North
Would ultimately bring on a brutal Civil War
Negro rights of citizenship would not be the issue
And insuring Negroes rights would not cause the war

Racist America despicable slave practices
Mocked America's sacred Bill of Rights
It divided white America and angered Negroes
As a disgruntled America prepared to fight

The American Civil War was inevitable
Because keeping men in bondage is un-Godly and wrong
Servitude and slave labor, the Civil War did not settle
But, the Civil War resolved that **slave owners be dethroned**

John R. Davison

"BUS DRIVER"

A city bus intended to seat twenty passengers
Squeezes thirty passengers tightly inside
Children are bundled to their mother's back
The moving bus sways from side to side

The driver stares straight ahead
As the fare collecting busboy does his thing
Ushering passengers quickly on and off the bus
While from the door opening he leans and swings

He announces stops
He collects the fares
He controls the seating
And folds and unfolds the chairs

He speaks several dialects and languages
And he uses many hand signs
And he always signals the bus driver
Of the bus stop place and stopping time

Usually he is an adolescent
The busboy is quick and he is trim
He entertains the passengers
He is whimsical and has a charming grin

The driver switches lanes abruptly
He forgets to signal that he will turn
His passengers screech in their seats
The bus skids and almost overturns

In taking a curve
The driver looses control
His bus swerves suddenly this time
Causing him to skid off the road

As the bus skids, it crosses into another lane
Heading towards an oncoming car
The driver tries to pull back in time
But, realizes that he is over to far

He collides head on into a vehicle
Disheveled passengers scream and cringe
The bus driver knows that his career as a driver
Has come to a sudden and abrupt end

John R. Davison

"A COUP"

Church going folks I come to know in Africa
I found, like churchgoers everywhere
They attend worship to embrace the fellowship
And band together in unity and prayer

African Ministers preach to the governed
But, their sermons never criticize the government
But, churchgoers criticize all that is said
With a loud hallelujah, aha and Amen

Churchgoers won't publicly denounce Officials
And they won't criticize the Officials abuses
They passively succumb to bureaucratic blunders
And are left neglected and confused

The governed know their African Head of State
As a Dictator and Ruler, who's a Potentate?
One who will freely censure what they say
And rigidly control them in extraordinary ways

Few seemed surprised when the masses rebelled
When the masses violently demanded their due
The masses plundered, assassinated and many died
And the world called, the regime's takeover a **Coup**

"OLD PA"

In Africa, to be called Ole Pa
Means that you are special to a lad
It means you are central in the lad's life
Like the father he once had

I clearly remember the Sunday
When I visited the Church nearby
That Sunday I inherited an entire family
Much to my dismay and surprise

The family visited after worship service
Their mother, the proud mother of ten
And as she was about to leave my home
She promised she'd visit me again

Again, she delayed her departure
And she turned to me and said
You need help with this great big house
My nephew needs a job and his own bed

My nephew knows how to manage a house
And he will work hard for his stay
You won't have to pay him very much
And he won't get in your way

Next month, he can move in with you
Next week, you should let him start
Meanwhile, my son Richard will stop by
And help you maintain your large yard

I allowed her nephew to have the job
And I also saw Richard, more and more
Both cousins completely ran the house
And I was relieved of domestic chores

Richard, her teenage son played soccer well
Richard was agile, precise and smooth
His distance kick, was powerful and quick
And he always followed through

Sunday, after a soccer game
Richard complained of feeling sick
His eyes were closed as he fell to the floor
Richard was having a seizure and fit

Within a matter of minutes
Richard was up and he was fine
Then he calmly told me
This happens from time to time

I had not been aware
That this lad who looked in on me
As sixteen, was on medication
To control his epilepsy

Richard's father, the Ambassador, was my neighbor
I was told, he had served worldwide
But, now remarried with a young wife and baby
This Ambassador to Sweden was rarely around

Richard's mom seemed to manage somehow
Without the security once taken for granted
Her kids, mostly adult, worked and helped out
But, she still had a hard time with ten kids about

Richard stopped by after the April 14th **Coup**
I could tell by his eyes, he was very sad
During the Coup soldiers had raped his Dad's wife
And had shot his father in the head

Richard said to me
As he quietly sobbed
You know that this means
You are now my '**Ole Pa**'

"FAREWELL"

I will never forget Africa
Or the friendships I have made
My fond memories of Africa
Will not ever fade

To my beloved Africa
I shall always remain
A devout supporter
Of all your legitimate claims

God created the world and all within it
And God is the Creator of all mankind
And the dominion He entrusts to his created
Is just as much yours, as mine

Africans right to a good life
The right to Peace and National dignity
God, Himself destined for Africa
And it remains within her reach

My stay in Africa
Confirmed my avowed belief
That we are all God's children
Born to be equal and free

John R. Davison

EXAMING A WORKER WITH A SEVERE NECK ACHE

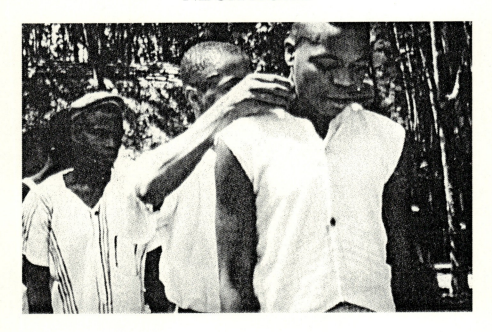

Tribal Midwives – Midwives practice the old way of caring for the sick.

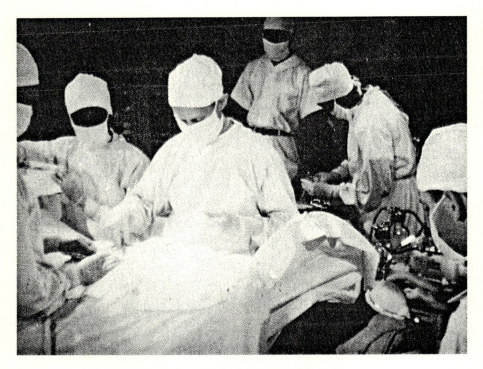

Surgery in a tribal clinic

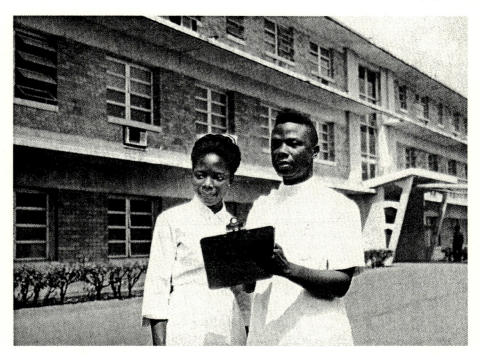

John R. Davison

A GATHERING OF VILLAGE PEOPLE

Women catch minnows (fish) in homemade baskets

Mandingo Acrobatic Dancers perform for villagers

Solid rubber being processed at the rubber plantation plant

A convergence of workers rubber tappers marching, enroute to the rubber plantation

Workers processing natural rubber to export as liquid latex

FOREIGN MINERS IN AFRICA

Drilling Crews building the Harbour

RUBBER: Planting havea seed in the Plantation Nursery

A 6,200 feet long Harbor to influence the world is completed

John R. Davison

Rubber Tree

MARKET PLACE–DOWNTOWN MONROVIA

John R. Davison

BLACK SMITHS
BASSA TRIBE

ABOUT THE AUTHOR

John R. Davison resides in Stone Mountain, Georgia just outside of Atlanta. He states that having entered the 21st Century, the new millennium, as a five year Association of American Retired Persons (AARP) card holding member, that be knows that he has been blessed by God and continues to be abundantly blessed and in God's favor.

John holds college degrees from two major universities. He holds a Bachelor of Science Degree in Business Administration received from Temple University and a Master of Science Degree in Management received from the University of Utah. He is certified fluent in French having completed the study program at the Army Language School. He is an accomplished classical pianist and lover of classical music. He worked as a Commissioned IRS Treasury Agent and served as an Accountant & Internal Auditor with the Opportunities Industrialization Centers, Inc. where he worked collaboratively with a prominent Certified Public Accounting firm. He served as a NASD licensed Securities Dealer with The Prudential brokering their variable investment products, he served as a Bank Executive with Fidelity Bank in both the Trust and Estate Division and bank float system. He served as the Operational Director and Financial Officer for multi-million dollar Trade Union Training Center.

John's education, training and affluence has enabled him to travel all over the world. John has traveled to and worked in the Carribean, seen most of Europe, South America and he spent two years in Foreign Service as a professional stationed in Liberia, West Africa where he provided technical assistance on various levels. After completing his tour in Africa, he returned home to the United States and five years later completed his first book, entitled 'A Poetic Glimpse of Africa.'

John states that A Poetic Glimpse of Africa was originally a manuscript for a book. However, he chose to transpose the manuscript into a poetic book which proved to be an awesome undertaking. The book will allow you to journey back in time with him to the years he lived in Africa and the journey will acquaint you with the culture and folkways of the Africa people he came to know and love. His collection of writings and poetic works number four to date and they touch upon various aspects of his life's experiences. However, given the uniqueness of his experiences in Africa he wanted his first book to be enlightening, educational and entertaining which lends to the book's poetic format.

John was born the third son of a poor young African-American couple who were illiterate sharecroppers. He would be a first in his family and first in his generation to graduate college and achieve a modicum of success. John knew little of his biological parents as a youngsters and he was well into his late teens when he met his biological mother the first time. John never knew or met his biological father. He left rural Georgia with his maternal Aunt Nina and her husband Tom when he was only three months old.

It has been quite a journey from that point to this point. John's fourth book entitled "From Sharecropper to CEO Shareholder" reveals his life's story from then to now. The fourth book will hopefully be released in 2003. John's maternal aunt Nina and his aunt's husband Tom relocated to Philadelphia. It was there where he received his education and he resided in Philadelphia until November of 1999 when he relocated to Atlanta. When John was sixteen years old his Aunt Nina suffered a massive and fatal stroke. Literally orphaned, John accepted Tom's married daughter Betty's invitation to remain with her family. John always worked and paid board when his mother was living, so he continued to work and continued to pay board to his sister, Betty and completed High School. His hard working mindset and focus paid off in spite of the many obstacles he faced. In time he became well educated, invested wisely an earned a modicum of financial success. John currently resides in Atlanta, in Georgia the state of his birth and serves as the United States Department of Labor's Bureau Director for Georgia.

John states, that to God he gives all the Glory, Honor and Praise.

Printed in the United States
1448200005B/10-33